Binaural Beats:

Sound Healing, Hypnosis, Lucid Dreaming & Restorative Sleep. Discover Spiritual Awakening and Powerful Meditation. Delta Waves to Reduce Stress and Improve Weight Loss

By EasyTube Zen Studio

© Copyright 2021 by EasyTube Zen Studio. All right reserved.

The work contained herein has been produced with the intent to provide relevant knowledge and information on the topic on the topic described in the title for entertainment purposes only. While the author has gone to every extent to furnish up to date and true information, no claims can be made as to its accuracy or validity as the author has made no claims to be an expert on this topic. Notwithstanding, the reader is asked to do their own research and consult any subject matter experts they deem necessary to ensure the quality and accuracy of the material presented herein.

This statement is legally binding as deemed by the Committee of Publishers Association and the American Bar Association for the territory of the United States. Other jurisdictions may apply their own legal statutes. Any reproduction, transmission or copying of this material contained in this work without the express written consent of the copyright holder shall be deemed as a copyright violation as per the current legislation in force on the date of publishing and subsequent time thereafter. All additional works derived from this material may be claimed by the holder of this copyright.

The data, depictions, events, descriptions and all other information forthwith are considered to be true, fair and accurate unless the work is expressly described as a work of fiction. Regardless of the nature of this work, the Publisher is exempt from any responsibility of actions taken by the reader in conjunction with this work. The Publisher acknowledges that the reader acts of their own accord and releases the author and Publisher of any responsibility for the observance of tips, advice, counsel, strategies and techniques that may be offered in this volume.

NEW Soothing Sounds for Deep Sleep Available NOW

Click the Links on Next Page to Download it NOW

Chapter 1

"Nowhere can a man find a quieter or more untroubled retreat than his own soul."

Marcus Aurelius

In the hustle and bustle of modern life, it can feel easy to lose contact with ourselves. Between balancing our work lives with our social lives, our list of external obligations can make it nearly impossible to find time to turn our attention inward—and this can take a physical toll on our bodies. Whether it takes the form of weight gain, sleep loss, or some other malady, disconnecting from our body's needs—both physical and spiritual—will eventually have effects that can be catastrophic.

Simply put, if we don't make time for our wellness, then we will inevitably be forced to make time for our illness. However, you do have the power to reframe the narrative. You can take control of your health before things reach a critical level and demand your attention. One of the best ways you can begin to create harmony and balance for your mind, body, and soul is by incorporating meditation into your daily routine.

A growing focus among advocates of meditation is something known as transcendental meditation. Originating in India in the 1950s, this style of meditation focuses on detaching oneself from negative energies like anxiety, depression, and even grief while focusing on promoting a sense of peace and harmony that can help the meditator with self-realization and self-actualization.

Among myriad other tools that can be used to assist with transcendental meditation—such as metaphysical supplies like sage or crystals, which have become popular among the New Age community—many transcendental meditators have begun incorporating something known as binaural beats into their spiritual routine to assist with things like lucid dreaming, spiritual healing, weight loss, and stress reduction.

What Are Binaural Beats?

Before we get into the various applications of binaural beats, it's important to understand what they are and how they work on a scientific level. In essence, a binaural beat is a kind of illusion that is created by your brain—this is done by playing two different tones at different frequencies in each ear. When this happens, your brain interprets the sound as a third tone—the binaural beat.

What is really happening when you hear these two tones is that your brain is resolving the frequency difference between the two tones as a single tone. For example, if one tone is played at 300Hz, while the other is played at 310Hz, the binaural beat that is created is 10hz because it represents the difference between these two tones.

The perception of this sound is created by the same portion of the brain that typically works to locate sounds in our environment. Because it requires two different tones to be played at two different hertz in each ear, if you were to remove your earphone from a single ear, you would no longer be able to hear the 10hz binaural beat and would instead hear the single tone at its normal hertz.

What Do Binaural Beats Do?

Binaural beats have a wide variety of purposes. Research into this auditory phenomenon shows that it has immense therapeutic benefits. This is because the binaural beat created by two different tones has been shown to tap into different parts of our brains depending on the hertz of each tone.

Every frequency is correlated with a different brain wave activity, and these are typically grouped into a range of patterns. Broadly speaking, these patterns include gamma, beta, alpha, theta, and delta. You should select a binaural beat with a frequency that corresponds to whatever it is you're trying to accomplish through meditation.

- **Gamma:** This is the highest frequency that your brain is capable of perceiving. It generally sits between 30Hz and 50Hz. Binaural beats played at this tone are associated with things like improved memory, alertness, concentration, and executive functioning. An ideal binaural beat for tapping into the gamma frequency is around 40Hz—this will help you experience most of the positive effects of this frequency.

- **Beta:** The beta pattern frequency typically sits between 13Hz and 30Hz. Like the gamma frequency, beta frequency waves are typically associated with high activity in the brain and help trigger alertness. Likewise, high levels of beta waves in the brain can be associated with things like hypervigilance and anxiety. Listening to beats at this frequency can help improve productivity, as well as memory and accuracy when performing tasks.

- **Alpha:** Bringing things down a little over the previous two patterns, the alpha pattern vibrates at a frequency between 8Hz and 13Hz. This one is associated with putting the mind at rest, and meditators can listen to this frequency if they want an improved sense of relaxation or to help tap into their creative mind. As an example, someone suffering from writer's block may wish to listen to binaural beats vibrating at this frequency to help unlock their abilities.

- **Theta:** Things are now winding down to the lowest frequency, with theta waves only vibration between 4Hz and 8Hz. This is the brain wave produced by the brain during the first stage of the sleep cycle, which also happens to be the lightest stage. Listening to binaural beats that vibrate at this frequency can be used to help with quiet, introspective meditation. This vibration can also be used to promote better sleep and relaxation.

- **Delta:** The lowest frequency the brain can perceive, delta waves vibrate at a frequency between 0.5Hz and 4Hz. Our brains produce delta waves when we enter into a state of deep sleep, known as rapid eye movement (REM). This frequency can be used to help enter a state of deep sleep or simply one of the deepest levels of relaxation. It can be a powerful tool for meditation, as well as helping you tap into the part of your brain associated with creativity and dreaming, as well as aiding in stress reduction.

Chapter Summary

Now that we've covered some of the scientific details of how binaural beats work, as well as which frequencies are associated with various parts of the brain, we can now start to unpack some of the real-world applications of these powerful tones. In the next chapter, we will go over some of the ways you can use binaural beats to promote things like better sleep, weight loss, relaxation, stress reduction, lucid dreaming, and more.

Chapter 2

"Ask for what you want and be prepared to get it."

Maya Angelou

Many of us live with burdens that we do not express. Whether it's something as simple as going about our day at the office in a haze because we suffer from chronic insomnia, or something more complex like the pain of past trauma and repressed memories that we haven't resolved continuing to wreak havoc on our lives as adults, many of these issues can—and should—be resolved with professional therapy from licensed counselors. However, the benefits of a more holistic approach cannot be underestimated.

For thousands of years, our ancestors lived without the power of modern medicine. As evidenced by our existence, they managed to find ways to continue to survive in sometimes harsh and unforgiving conditions. This required them to live their lives closely intertwined with both the natural world and the spiritual world.

Regardless of whether you consider yourself a religious person or not, the research into the immense benefits of things like meditation and binaural beats proves that these practices have validity. Whether you choose to incorporate them into your life as part of a broader spiritual journey or simply based on the abundance of literature on the subject proving their viability doesn't really matter—what matters is the tremendous effect these techniques can have on your physical and mental well-being.

Applications of Binaural Beats

Binaural beats have a wide range of applications that make them an immensely useful tool for anyone looking to step up their meditation and even those looking to achieve specific results from their meditative practice. As we discussed in the previous chapter, different wave patterns tap into different parts of the brain.

Likewise, if you're looking to accomplish a certain goal, you should listen to beats that align with that portion of your brain. Some of the things that can be achieved with binaural beats include sound healing, hypnosis, lucid dreaming, restorative sleep, weight loss, and stress reduction.

- **Sound Healing:** One of the most incredible things that can be accomplished with binaural beats is their ability to help recover memories of past trauma. If you suffer from repressed memories, you will likely want to tap into the gamma wave frequency, which is strongly associated with memory and improved cognition. This should be done in a therapeutic setting so you can help resolve memories as they arise in a safe and healthy manner.

  If you already work with a therapist, you should consider asking them about incorporating binaural beats into your treatment plan. Some therapists may not be familiar with this treatment method, so you may either refer them to the literature on the subject or consult with a mental health professional who already includes binaural beats in their practice.

- **Hypnosis:** Many hypnotherapists incorporate binaural beats into their practice. Like all binaural beats, the vibration frequency of the beat will vary based on what you're trying to achieve with hypnotherapy. Be sure to talk with a qualified therapist about which wavelength will work best for you, depending on what it is you're trying to accomplish with hypnosis.

It's important that you work with an experienced professional before seeking out any form of hypnosis or hypnotherapy, as this practice can do more harm than good in an unstructured setting.

- **Lucid Dreaming:** One of the most appealing things binaural beats can help you achieve is lucid dreaming, sometimes referred to by those in the spiritual community as astral projection—although some people will make distinctions between the two phenomena. Compared to other items on this list, this one is less about personal growth and discovery and more about fun—however, spiritualists will tell you this is an extremely sacred exploration of the astral plane with immense learning opportunities.

One of the best ways to achieve a state of lucid dreaming is to create a playlist that includes two different frequencies. Begin by playing binaural beats in the theta wave frequency to simulate a state of deep sleep. Next, have the transition of the wave to the gamma frequency to increase your cognition, thereby creating the intended "mind awake, body asleep" effect.

- **Restorative Sleep:** Many people turn to binaural beats as a last resort to address insomnia. Many of the pharmaceuticals associated with preventing insomnia are not intended for long-term use due to their side effects and strong addiction potential. Instead, you can incorporate binaural beats into your sleep routine to help with falling asleep and staying asleep through the night.

  The best way to accomplish this is by using binaural beats that vibrate at the theta and delta frequencies. These are proven to help us enter a deepened state of relaxation, promoting better, more restful, dreamless sleep. This can also help with preventing nightmares, night terrors, and sleep paralysis.

- **Weight Loss:** One of the best ways to promote weight loss with binaural beats is by increasing your activity level. The primary method you can use to accomplish this is by regularly listening to binaural beats that vibrate at the gamma frequency. These can be listened to before a workout or even during to maximize your energy levels.

  Beta waves can be used to accomplish a similar effect. Making these beats a part of your daily life will leave you looking forward to your next workout, and the increase of dopamine you will experience as a result will have a measurable impact on your sense of well-being.

- **Stress Reduction:** This one can be thought of as the inversion of weight loss—rather than trying to raise your activity level and alertness, you will want to bring things down a few notches. The best way to do this is by listening to binaural beats vibrating at the lowest frequency vibrations—theta and delta.

  These have been clinically demonstrated to not only help promote better sleep but also increase feelings of relaxation and stress reduction.

Chapter Summary

Now that you have a better understanding of some of the myriad ways in which you can use binaural beats to achieve real-life goals, we can move on to the next chapter, where we will discuss some of the actual means by which you can use these tones for an intended purpose.

Chapter 3

In the first two chapters, we unpacked how binaural beats worked and some of the ways they can be used—including recovering repressed memories, lucid dreaming improving sleep, and even achieving physical benefits, such as weight loss. In this chapter, we will talk about some of the ways that you do each of these, either at home or in a therapeutic setting.

Sound Healing

While using binaural beats to explore things like repressed memories is best reserved for the structured setting of a qualified therapist's office, there are other methods of using the beats as a part of your spiritual healing journey that can safely be practiced from your own home.

The practice of sound healing goes back to the ancient Mediterranean, where the Greeks, Romans, and Egyptians used music to help cure mental disorders, in addition to using music as a method of mood improvement. Given the fact the human body is 75% water and water is a scientifically proven conductor of sound vibrations, it's no wonder the human body responds so well to this form of therapy. Some of the benefits include the following:

- Decreased Stress Levels

- Decreased Mood Volatility
- Decrease in Blood Pressure
- Lower Cholesterol

To use binaural beats to tap into the healing properties of sound, we recommend carving out a daily allotment of time that you dedicate purely to your sound therapy practice. Find a space that is dimly lit and quiet. Be sure to turn off notifications on your devices and let anyone with whom you share your space know that you don't wish to be disturbed for your chosen period of time.

This can range anywhere from 15 minutes to start to up to an hour a day if you're able to make time. The amount of time you dedicate to your sound healing practice is not nearly as the quality of each session. Be sure to find a space where you can lay down comfortably and use high-quality earphones turned up to medium volume—any higher, and you'll risk damage to your delicate eardrums.

Hypnosis

Like sound healing, there are some components of hypnosis—like recalling repressed memories—that are best left to therapeutic environments. Regardless of what it is you're trying to accomplish, hypnosis should only be undertaken with the assistance of someone you trust to help guide you through the journey and stay close to make sure you don't act out while hypnotized, potentially harming yourself or others.

For those who are seeking out hypnosis as part of a spiritual journey, you may wish to use the services of a practiced shaman or another spiritual guide who is experienced in ritualistic hypnosis, but be sure to find one who already incorporates binaural beats into their practice for the best possible results. Some of the benefits of hypnosis include the following:

- Decreased Anxiety
- Soothing Irritable Bowel Syndrome (IBS)
- Decrease in Chronic Pain
- Help in Quitting Smoking

As always, find a relaxing place where you and your chosen hypnosis sitter can be comfortable for the duration of the session. One of the best ways to achieve hypnosis at home with binaural beats is by listening to a guided meditation with binaural beats included as background noise.

Typically, the voice track will use subliminal messaging that's tailored to what it is you're trying to accomplish. Additionally, the frequency of the vibration will depend on what it is you're trying to accomplish with hypnosis. For instance, if you want to quit smoking, listening to beats in the gamma frequency—around 30Hz—will help you tap into the part of the brain associated with better executive functioning, helping you exert more control over your habits.

Lucid Dreaming

Lucid dreaming is closely related to—and sometimes used interchangeably with—out-of-body experiences (OBE) and astral projection, but it's important to note that the phenomena all have distinctions that make them separate from one another, albeit closely related.

For starters, most lucid dreamers do not consider the experience as anything more than being aware during their dreams, allowing them to be active participants who can control their actions and the outcomes of the dream, rather than simply watching their dreams unfold as is typical in a normal state of dreaming.

Astral projection is considered by practitioners to be a spiritual experience in which their spirit leaves their body and enters the astral plane. For those in the spiritual community, this experience is neither a dream nor a hallucination—it is a literal departure of the astral body from the physical body and is considered a profoundly spiritual phenomenon.

Both lucid dreamers and astral projectors incorporate binaural beats into their practice—both work by using similar methods. The idea is to trick the body into falling asleep while the mind remains awake. The best way to do this with binaural beats is starting with low-frequency vibrations that transition to high-frequency vibrations halfway through the track.

First, find a quiet place where you can relax without being disturbed. This place should be comfortable and dimly lit, and you should give yourself ample time to allow yourself to enter a state of deep relaxation—be sure to have a schedule that is clear several hours in advance to avoid any potential distraction.

While you allow your body to relax, focus your mind on thoughts of expansion. Picture your awareness as a light that starts in your mind and grows outward, extending beyond your body. As you do this, you may select a track with vocals that help you along your journey. As with any discipline, lucid dreaming and astral projection take practice—don't be discouraged if you don't succeed on your first attempt.

Restorative Sleep

Many medical doctors and therapists field complaints from patients who say they have trouble sleeping and that traditional medications either have too many side effects don't work properly, or worked but eventually became ineffective after the patient fell into a cycle of tolerance and dependency. In the latter cases, patients may even find their insomnia is worse than before with their medication and that sleep has become impossible without it.

Because of this, patients often resort to holistic methods of getting better, more consistent sleep. Common options include natural medicines like melatonin, but many patients have excellent outcomes with sound therapy. This can include white noise, soothing music, and binaural beats.

For the most optimized outcome with binaural beats, it's best to start by practicing good sleep hygiene. This may mean cutting out some bad habits and investing in your sleep space. No more falling asleep on the couch. Bad mattress? Replace it. Bright lights that seep in through your bedroom's blinds? Buy some blackout curtains.

Be sure you are always falling asleep in a room that is dark, quiet, and cool. It is better to sleep in a room that is a lower temperature than what you would find comfortable and layer yourself with blankets rather than sleep in a space that is too warm. Many patients find that weighted blankets have an immensely therapeutic effect.

Invest in a pair of comfortable, noise-canceling headphones. For most patients, the best sleep position to optimize restful sleep is flat on one back. You should create a playlist that includes various tracks in the theta and delta frequency range.

The best approach is, to begin with, theta—around 4Hz to 8Hz—and listen to this for the first 30 minutes, allowing your body to enter a stay of relaxation before transitioning to delta frequency vibrations which will help you achieve deep sleep.

Weight Loss & Stress Reduction

The two most optimal ways of achieving weight loss and stress reduction are by following the same techniques that were laid out in the portion of this chapter, where we discussed sound healing and hypnosis. It may sound difficult to believe that binaural beats can be used to achieve both of these goals, but the science on the subject is clear.

Sound therapy and hypnosis with binaural beats both act in a similar manner—decreasing stress by creating a space in your life for gentle relaxation while using binaural beats to connect with brainwaves that promote a sense of well-being and mindfulness. This will pay off in dividends when it comes to both physical and mental health, and those who are using binaural beats as part of their spiritual journey will experience immense growth in this area as well.

The best way to experience all the benefits binaural beats have to offer is by making them a part of your daily life. You can't expect to shed pounds after a single session—it must be an ongoing discipline that you create time for, even if it takes time to start seeing results. Begin by listening to 15 minutes of binaural beats in the gamma frequency every day, with a guided meditation vocal track that focuses on weight loss, self-realization, and self-actualization.

You can even listen to these in your office at work. Simply tell your coworkers that you will be taking time for lunch and find an area where you will not be disturbed. You don't need to close your eyes, but you may do so if you wish. While lying down is preferable, this type of meditation is more active and can be practiced in an upright position.

Throughout the day, be sure to reaffirm the messages you focused on in your session—these will usually follow similar themes, which can generally be summarized as follows: you are worthy, and you have the power to achieve your goals.

Conclusion

We hope you enjoyed this book and found some of the information included useful. Whether you're a spiritual person or a skeptic, the powerful impact that binaural beats can have on our physical, mental, and emotional health is demonstrable and scientifically measurable.

Skeptics may wish to lean on the scientific literature on the subject, which proves that patient outcomes are improved when binaural beats are used to satisfy an intended purpose—like improved sleep or stress reduction—in therapeutic settings. Spiritualists will appreciate the ways in which binaural beats can aid things like astral projection and past life regression.

Binaural beats sit at the border between these two disciplines and show that they are not necessarily as out of alignment with one another as they may appear. The folk medicinal traditions of our ancestors—which included sound as a form of healing—helped keep our species alive for millennia. They are not as easily discounted as many people in our modern world would like you to believe.

Thank you for your purchase and for choosing to make this book a part of your journey—regardless of the unique path you're traveling on.

Thank You

Thank you so much for purchasing my book.

You could have picked from dozens of other books, but you picked our book Binaural Beats

So, THANK YOU for getting this book and for making it all the way to the end.

Before you go, I wanted to ask you for one small favour.

Could you please consider posting a review on the platform?

Posting a review is the best and easiest way to support the work of independent authors like me.

Your feedback will help me to keep writing the kind of books that will help you get the results you want. It would mean a lot to me to hear from you.

>> Leave a review on Amazon US <<

www.ingramcontent.com/pod-product-compliance
Lightning Source LLC
Chambersburg PA
CBHW050157130526
44590CB00044B/3371